CONTENTS

01 | **Allah** 06
02 | **Ar Rahman | Ar Raheem** 10
03 | **Al Malik** 14
04 | **Al Qudoos** 18
05 | **As Salaam** 22
06 | **Al Mu'min** 26
07 | **Al Muhaymin** 30
08 | **Al Azeez** 34
09 | **Al Jabbar** 38
10 | **Al Mutakabbir** 42
11 | **Al Khaliq** 46
12 | **Al Ghaffar** 50
13 | **Al Qahhar** 54
14 | **Ar Razzaq** 58
15 | **Al Fattah** 62
16 | **Al Aleem** 66
17 | **At Tawaab** 70
18 | **Al Mujeeb** 74
19 | **Al Kareem** 78
20 | **Ar Rub** 82
21 | **Al Lateef** 86
22 | **Al Hakeem** 90
23 | **As Samee** 94
24 | **Al Haleem** 98
25 | **Ar Raqeeb** 102
26 | **Al Wadud** 106
27 | **Al Waasi** 110
28 | **Ar Rauf | Al Jami** 114
29 | **Al Haq** 118
30 | **Al Hameed** 122

Reward Chart

Dearest viewers, welcome to your new workbook!

There are 30 worksheets you need to complete, you can find the answers for each worksheet based on every episode of The Azharis. Each worksheet will help you learn a new name of Allah which will help you make your duas that extra bit special.

Colour in each circle once you have successfully completed the worksheet.

Episode 01
Allah

Episode 02
Ar Rahman & Ar Raheem

Episode 03
Al Malik

Episode 04
Al Qudoos

Episode 05
As Salaam

Episode 06
Al Mu'min

Episode 07
Al Muhaymin

Episode 08
Al Azeez

Episode 09
Al Jabbar

Episode 10
Al Mutakabbir

Episode 11
Al Khaliq

Episode 12
Al Ghaffar

Episode 13
Al Qahhar

Episode 14
Ar Razzaq

Episode 15
Al Fattah

Episode 16
Al Aleem

Episode 17
At Tawaab

Episode 18
Al Mujeeb

Episode 19
Al Kareem

Episode 20
Ar Rub

Episode 21
Al Lateef

Episode 22
Al Hakeem

Episode 23
As Samee

Episode 24
Al Jabbar

Episode 25
Ar Raqeeb

Episode 26
Al Wadud

Episode 27
Al Waasi

Episode 28
Ar Rauf & Al Jami

Episode 29
Al Haq

Episode 30
Al Hameed

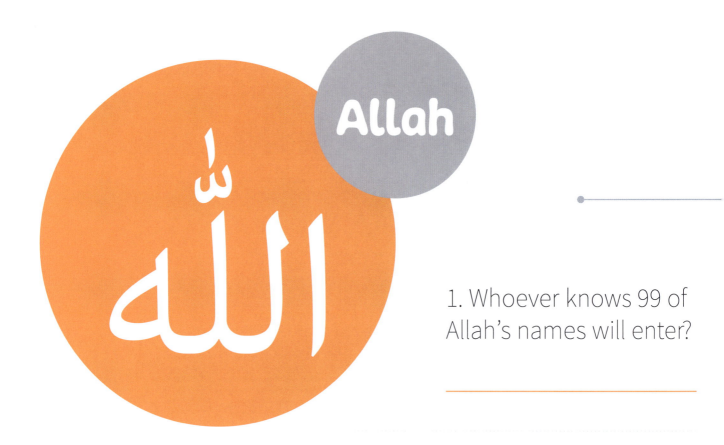

1. Whoever knows 99 of Allah's names will enter?

_____

2. Can there be more than one Allah?

Colour in the correct answer

3. What are the two names Allah loves most?

Tick the correct answers

- ○ Abdullah
- ○ Musa
- ○ Yahya
- ○ Esa
- ○ Abdul Rahman
- ○ Muhammad

4. What is the first surah in the Qur'an?

Join the dots

EPISODE 01

5. How many times is the name "Allah" mentioned in the Qur'an?

Circle the correct answer

Over 2,000   Over 20,000   Over 200

6. Before we eat what do we say?

Tick the correct answer and colour in

○ Alhamdulilah
○ Subhan'Allah
○ Bismillah

Don't forget to colour in your badge on completion of this worksheet

7. What is the dua for when you enter your home?

Colour in

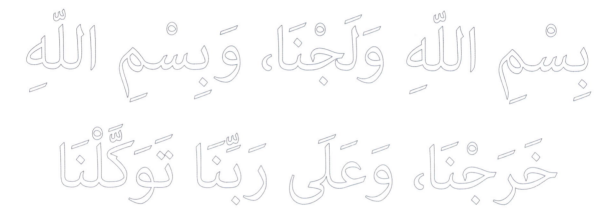

Bismillaahi walajnaa, wa bismillaahi kharajnaa, wa 'alaa Rabbinaa tawakkalnaa

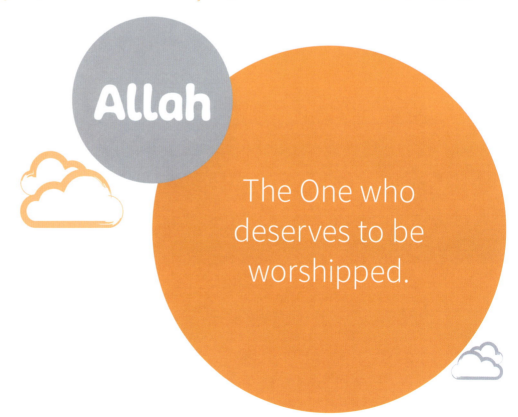

Allah

The One who deserves to be worshipped.

EPISODE 01

Wordsearch

Tick off the words as you find them

- ○ ALLAH
- ○ SURAH
- ○ BISMILLAH
- ○ DUA
- ○ QURAN
- ○ JANNAH

A	B	J	S	U	R	A	H	R
L	S	U	A	Z	Z	A	N	T
L	R	M	K	N	X	A	E	A
A	L	U	N	V	N	O	P	C
H	W	Y	B	A	O	A	M	D
L	U	T	R	H	J	E	H	U
I	K	U	P	N	N	A	Y	A
H	Q	A	M	A	O	I	R	C
B	I	S	M	I	L	L	A	H

Ar Rahman
Ar Raheem

الرَّحْمٰنُ
الرَّحِيْمِ

1. Which name means 'The Most Merciful'?

Draw a line to the correct answer

The Most Merciful

Ar Rahman

Al Malik

Al Qudoos

2. Which name means 'The One that gives out the mercy'?

Join the dots

AR RAHEEM

3. What does mercy mean?

_____

_____

_____

4. Draw a picture to show how you can be merciful to others

The Azharis | Names of Allah 10

EPISODE 02

5. Which is greater - Allah's mercy or his anger?

Tick the correct answer

◯ Anger
◯ Mercy

6. How can we get Allah's mercy ?

Write the answer and colour in

_____

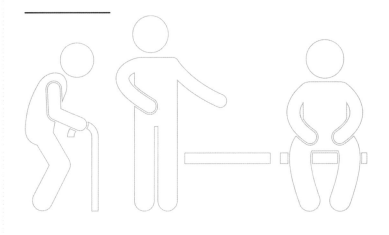

7. Is it good to share ?

Colour in the correct answer

8. Should we be kind to animals ?

Colour in the pictures and the correct answer

Don't forget to colour in your badge on completion of this worksheet

9. What was the story time about today?

_____

_____

_____

_____

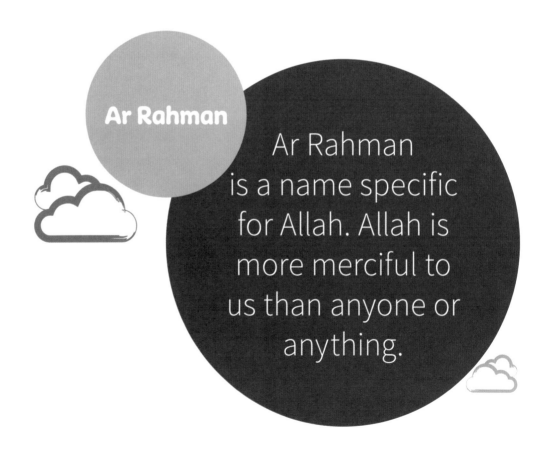

Ar Rahman

Ar Rahman is a name specific for Allah. Allah is more merciful to us than anyone or anything.

EPISODE 02

Wordsearch

Tick off the words as you find them

- ○ AR RAHMAN
- ○ MERCY
- ○ AR RAHEEM
- ○ ANGEL
- ○ KIND
- ○ SHARE

A	B	J	S	Y	O	D	B	U
D	R	U	C	Z	Z	A	N	T
P	R	R	K	A	N	G	E	L
A	E	U	A	V	I	O	P	K
M	W	Y	B	H	O	J	M	I
L	U	T	R	H	M	E	S	N
W	K	U	P	N	N	A	Y	D
S	H	A	R	E	O	I	N	C
A	A	R	R	A	H	E	E	M

The Azharis | Names of Allah 13

Al Malik

ٱلْمَلِكِ

1. What does Malik mean?

_____

2. At the time of Prophet Musa who thought they were the King of everything?

Colour in

3. When you give in charity what does an Angel do?

Write the answer and colour in

_____

_____

_____

4. When you give in charity, Allah will give you more back?

Colour in the correct answer

TRUE | FALSE

EPISODE 03

5. How many times do we say Subhan'Allah after we pray?

Tick the correct answer

○ 99
○ 66
○ 33

6. What surah do we recite on (Fridays?)

Circle the correct answer

Surah Al Baqarah

Surah Al Kahf

Surah Ya' Sin

7. Why was the rich man's garden destroyed?

_____
_____
_____
_____

Don't forget to colour in your badge on completion of this worksheet

8. Who is the King of Kings?
Colour in

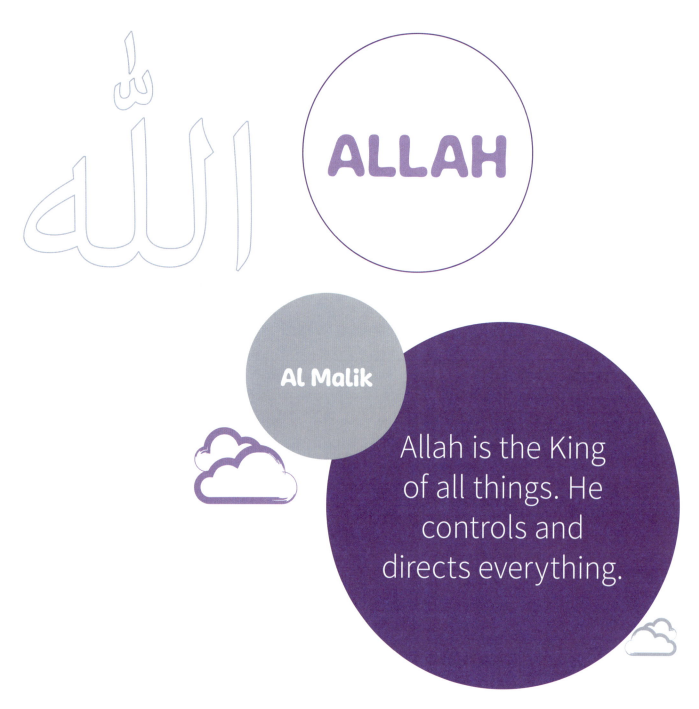

EPISODE 03

Wordsearch

Tick off the words as you find them

- ALLAH
- MALIK
- KING
- FIRAWN
- ANGEL
- CHARITY

F	B	D	A	L	L	A	H	F
R	S	U	A	Z	Z	A	N	T
L	F	I	R	A	W	N	F	A
K	L	U	N	V	K	O	P	N
I	A	Y	B	I	O	A	M	G
N	U	T	L	H	J	E	O	E
G	K	A	P	N	N	A	Y	L
H	M	A	M	A	O	I	R	C
K	F	C	H	A	R	I	T	Y

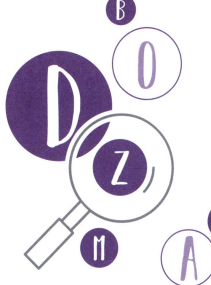

Al Qudoos

اَلْقُدُّوسُ

1. What does Al Qudoos mean?

Circle the correct answer

The King of Kings

The Most Merciful

The One that purifies

2. When you do a bad deed what colour dot is put on your heart?

_____

3. When you do a good deed should you tell people?

Colour in the correct answer

YES | NO

4. Which row has the most reward for men in the mosque?

Tick the correct answer

○ Middle
○ Front
○ Back

EPISODE 04

5. Is telling a lie good?
Colour in the correct answer

6. How did the Prophet Muhammad ﷺ treat people who were bad to him?

_____

_____

7. Which Prophet did the Prophet Muhammad ﷺ meet in the story time?
Join the dots

8. What did he say when he met him ﷺ?

_____

_____

_____

9. The other meaning of Al Qudoos is the One that?
Circle the correct answer

Puts barakah in things   Forgives you   Hears All

Don't forget to colour in your badge on completion of this worksheet

10. What would you like to have barakah in?

_____

_____

_____

_____

Al Qudoos

The One that purifies & puts barakah in things.

EPISODE 04

Wordsearch

Tick off the words as you find them

- ○ BARAKAH
- ○ AL QUDOOS
- ○ MUSA
- ○ LIE
- ○ PURE
- ○ MOSQUE

B	P	M	O	S	Q	D	B	U
D	A	U	E	Z	Z	A	M	S
P	R	R	K	E	N	G	O	L
A	U	U	A	V	I	O	S	M
P	W	Y	M	H	D	J	Q	O
L	U	T	R	U	P	E	U	L
I	K	U	Q	N	S	A	E	D
E	H	L	B	A	O	A	M	C
B	A	R	A	K	A	H	B	M

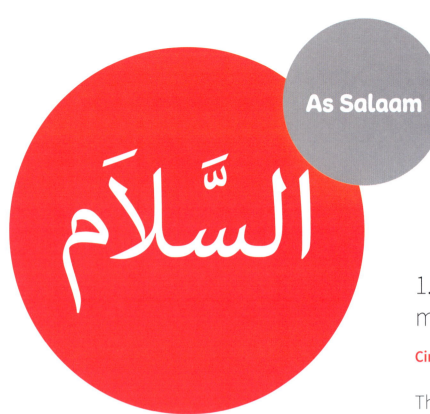

As Salaam

الـسَّلَام

1. What does As-Salaam mean?

Circle the correct answer

The Forgiver

The Protector

The All Hearing

2. What do you say when you meet someone?

Colour in

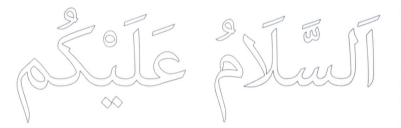

3. Who gets more reward, the one that starts this greeting or the one that returns it?

Tick the correct answer

○ Starts

○ Returns

EPISODE 05

4. How many gates are there to Jannah?

Join the dots

EIGHT

5. Can you give an example of being patient?

_____

_____

_____

_____

6. Draw a picture and let us know what you make du'a for.

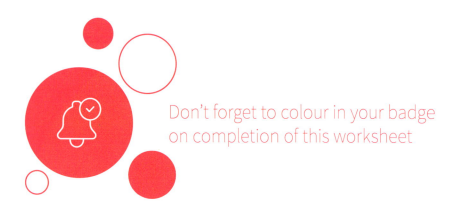

7. Which day should we send blessings on the Prophet Muhammad ﷺ more than others?

Circle the correct answer

Monday   Tuesday   Wednesday   Thursday   Friday

As Salaam

Allah is the One that protects us.

EPISODE 05

Wordsearch

Tick off the words as you find them

- ◯ JANNAH
- ◯ PATIENT
- ◯ AS SALAAM
- ◯ ALLAH
- ◯ FRIDAY
- ◯ DUA

F	J	J	U	N	L	P	H	F
R	S	U	A	Z	Z	A	A	P
D	F	I	L	N	U	N	Y	A
K	U	U	L	V	N	A	P	T
S	A	A	A	I	D	A	M	I
N	U	T	H	I	J	E	H	E
Z	K	A	R	N	N	A	Y	N
H	E	F	M	A	O	I	R	T
A	S	S	A	L	A	A	M	O

Al Mu'min

الْمُؤْمِن

1. What does Al Mu'min mean?

Circle the correct answer

The One who gives Eeman

The One who gives Patience

The One who gives Money

2. What is Qadr?

_____

3. Draw a picture and give an example of a good deed.

4. Who was the worst man ever?

Join the dots

EPISODE 06

5. What was the name of Firawn's wife?

Draw a line to the correct answer

Firawn

Asiyah

Khadijah

Mariam

6. What surah do we recite on Fridays?

Circle the correct answer

Surah Al Baqarah

Surah Al Kahf

Surah Ya'Sin

7. What was the name of Prophet Musa's brother?

Colour in

Don't forget to colour in your badge on completion of this worksheet

8. Who was with the Prophet Muhammad ﷺ in the cave?

Write the answer below and colour in

_____

Al Mu'min

Allah is the One that gives eeman and also protects us.

EPISODE 06

Wordsearch

Tick off the words as you find them

- ◯ EEMAN
- ◯ QADR
- ◯ FIRAWN
- ◯ SURAH KAHF
- ◯ MUSA
- ◯ HARUN

B	I	M	U	S	A	D	B	F
F	E	F	L	Z	Z	A	H	K
I	R	R	E	E	N	A	A	L
R	U	U	E	V	K	P	R	F
A	W	Y	M	H	Q	J	U	O
W	U	T	A	E	P	A	N	L
N	K	R	N	N	S	A	D	D
S	U	O	B	A	O	A	M	R
S	A	R	A	K	A	H	B	M

Al Muhaymin

الْمُهَيْمِن

1. What does Al Muhaymin mean?

Circle the correct answer

The One who Hears Everything

The One who Protects us

The One who Sees Everything

2. Which Prophet was in the belly of a whale?

Write the answer and colour in

_____

4. Which Prophet was put in a basket?

Write the answer and colour in

_____

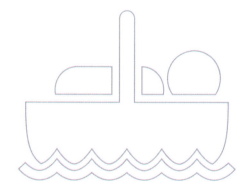

3. Which Prophet was thrown into a fire?

Write the answer and colour in

_____

The Azharis | Names of Allah 30

EPISODE 07

5. Which country did this happen in?

Write the answer and colour in

_____

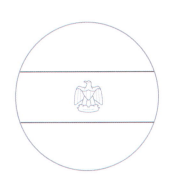

6. How many times do we pray a day?

Tick the correct answer

○ 5
○ 10
○ 3

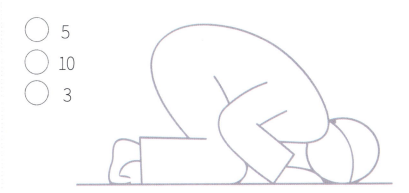

7. What happened when Prophet Yunus went on the boat?

_____

_____

_____

_____

Don't forget to colour in your badge on completion of this worksheet

8. Who else heard the dua of Prophet Yunus?
Circle the correct answer

Birds   Shaytan   Angels

Al Muhaymin

Allah is forever watching over us.

EPISODE 07

Wordsearch

Tick off the words as you find them

- ALLAH
- YUNUS
- MUSA
- IBRAHIM
- ANGELS
- EGYPT

F	J	I	U	N	L	P	H	F
I	S	E	G	Y	P	T	A	A
O	B	I	A	N	G	E	L	S
K	U	R	L	A	N	A	P	T
S	A	A	A	I	L	A	M	I
N	U	T	I	H	J	L	H	E
M	U	S	A	N	I	A	A	N
H	E	F	M	A	O	M	R	H
B	W	S	Y	U	N	U	S	O

The Azharis | Names of Allah 33

Al Azeez

الْعَزِيزُ

1. What does Al Azeez mean?

Circle the correct answer

The Most Powerful

The Most Patient

The Most Caring

2. Is there anyone more powerful than Allah?

Colour in the correct answer

YES | NO

3. Which Prophet called the birds and they came back to life?

Write the answer and colour in

_____

4. Which river was Prophet Musa placed in when he was a baby?

Write the answer and colour in

_____

EPISODE 08

5. Which country is this in?

Tick the correct answer

◯ Saudi Arabia
◯ Egypt
◯ Palestine

6. Which man did Prophet Musa go to?

Join the dots

7. When you love Allah, He will love you?

Colour in the correct answer

TRUE | FALSE

8. Which surah was mentioned in the episode with Al-Azeez?

Tick the correct answer

◯ Surah Ikhlas
◯ Surah Mulk
◯ Surah Baqarah

Al Azeez

Allah owns all honour and might. He alone can overpower anyone and anything.

Wordsearch

Tick off the words as you find them

- ◯ IBRAHIM
- ◯ MUSA
- ◯ BASKET
- ◯ NILE
- ◯ AL AZEEZ
- ◯ SURAH

B	I	M	U	S	I	D	B	F
M	U	S	A	Z	B	N	O	K
A	R	R	E	E	R	A	A	L
R	L	U	E	V	A	P	R	S
A	W	A	M	N	H	J	U	U
W	U	T	Z	E	I	U	N	R
N	K	R	N	E	M	L	D	A
S	U	O	B	A	E	A	E	H
B	A	S	K	E	T	Z	B	M

Al Jabbar

1. What does Al Jabbar mean?

Circle the correct answer

The One that Fixes

The One that Protects

The Most Merciful

2. How many times is the name Al Jabbar in the Quran?

Tick the correct answer

◯ 9
◯ 1
◯ 3

3. Is there anyone stronger than Allah?

Colour in the correct answer

4. How long were Prophet Musa's people banned for because they did not listen?

Circle the correct answer

40 Days

40 Months

40 Years

EPISODE 09

5. Who was the next Prophet mentioned in this episode?

Colour in

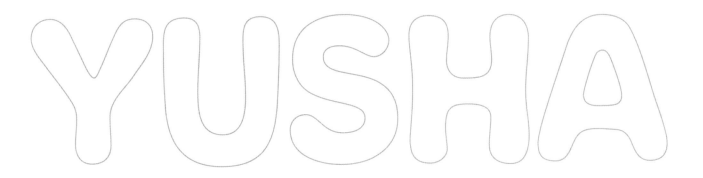

6. What did he make dua for?

Write the answer and colour in

_____

_____

_____

7. How did Prophet Yusha find the man who stole from the treasure?

_____
_____
_____
_____

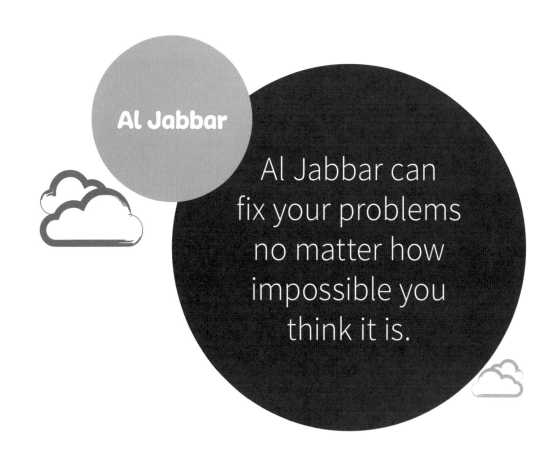

Al Jabbar

Al Jabbar can fix your problems no matter how impossible you think it is.

EPISODE 09

Wordsearch

Tick off the words as you find them

- ○ YUSHA
- ○ AL JABBAR
- ○ ALLAH
- ○ DUA
- ○ PRAY
- ○ PROPHET

P	P	Y	U	N	L	P	H	Y
R	S	R	G	K	P	T	A	U
O	B	I	O	N	G	A	L	S
K	U	R	L	P	N	A	L	H
S	A	Y	A	I	H	A	A	A
P	R	A	Y	H	J	E	H	E
K	E	S	A	N	I	A	T	N
H	A	L	J	A	B	B	A	R
B	W	S	D	U	A	K	S	O

The Azharis | Names of Allah 41

Al Mutakabbir

الْمُتَكَبِّر

1. What does Al Mutakabbir mean?
Circle the correct answer

The One who is the Greatest

The One that Protects

The King

2. What do you say to start your prayer?
Colour in

ALLAHUAKBAR

3. What does Allahuakbar mean?

_____

_____

_____

4. Who was the first Prophet?
Join the dots

ADAM

EPISODE 10

5. In the story of Prophet Adam who did not bow down?

Colour in

6. What hand should we eat with?

Tick the correct answer

○ Left
○ Right

7. Will Shaytan die?

Colour in the correct answer

8. What was Prophet Adam created from?

___

___

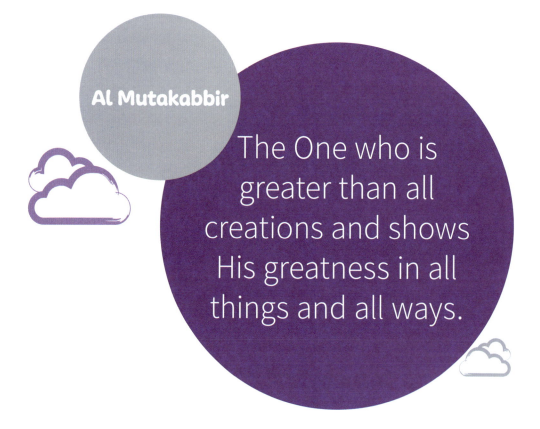

Al Mutakabbir

The One who is greater than all creations and shows His greatness in all things and all ways.

EPISODE 10

Wordsearch

Tick off the words as you find them

- ○ ADAM
- ○ SHAYTAN
- ○ PRAY
- ○ ANGELS
- ○ QURAN
- ○ ALLAH

E	I	A	U	S	I	A	B	F
N	U	N	E	Z	B	L	O	K
A	R	G	A	L	L	A	A	N
R	L	E	E	V	A	P	A	S
A	Q	L	M	N	H	T	D	U
P	U	S	Z	E	Y	U	A	S
N	R	R	N	A	M	L	M	A
S	A	A	H	A	E	A	E	L
B	N	S	Y	A	L	L	A	H

Al Khaliq

1. What does Al Khaliq mean?

Circle the correct answer

The Creator

The Protector

The Most Merciful

2. Who created the sun?

Write the answer and colour in

_____

3. The Quran gives life to our …

Tick the correct answer

○ Hearts
○ House
○ Food

4. The most beloved people to Allah are the most helpful to others?

Join the dots

EPISODE 11

5. Al Bari means the one that starts creating something out of nothing?

Colour in the correct answer

6. Al Musawir means the one that creates the fine details and brings everything together?

Colour in the correct answer

7. In which season do we get fruits in normally?

Tick the correct answer

- ◯ Spring
- ◯ Summer
- ◯ Autumn
- ◯ Winter

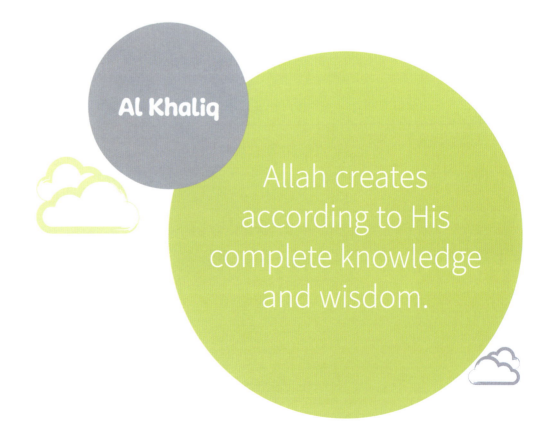

Al Khaliq

Allah creates according to His complete knowledge and wisdom.

EPISODE 11

Wordsearch

Tick off the words as you find them

- ○ AL KHALIQ
- ○ AL BARI
- ○ AL MUSAWIR
- ○ QURAN
- ○ TREE
- ○ JANNAH

P	P	Y	U	N	L	P	H	Q
J	S	R	G	K	P	T	A	U
A	L	M	U	S	A	W	I	R
N	U	R	L	P	N	I	L	A
N	A	Y	A	T	R	E	E	N
A	R	A	Y	A	J	E	O	E
H	E	S	B	N	I	A	T	N
H	A	L	B	A	B	B	A	R
B	A	L	K	H	A	L	I	Q

The Azharis | Names of Allah 49

Al Ghaffar

الْغَفَّار

1. Al Ghaffar refers to...

Circle the correct answer

The One who Protects

The One who Creates

The One who Forgives

2. If you do something wrong what should you do?

_____
_____

3. Is there a limit to how many times you can turn back to Allah ?

Colour in the correct answer

YES | NO

EPISODE 12

4. Who cried when a verse was revealed?

Tick the correct answer
- ◯ Firawn
- ◯ Shaytan
- ◯ Haman

5. Who ate from a tree by mistake?

Write the answer and colour in

_____

6. Draw a picture to show what you want to do in Jannah.

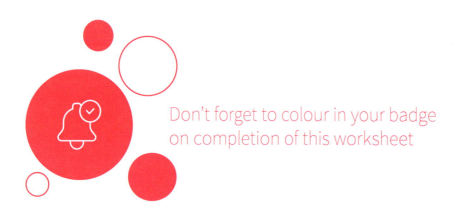

Don't forget to colour in your badge on completion of this worksheet

7. Which Prophet was involved in the story of the drought?
Join the dots

MUSA

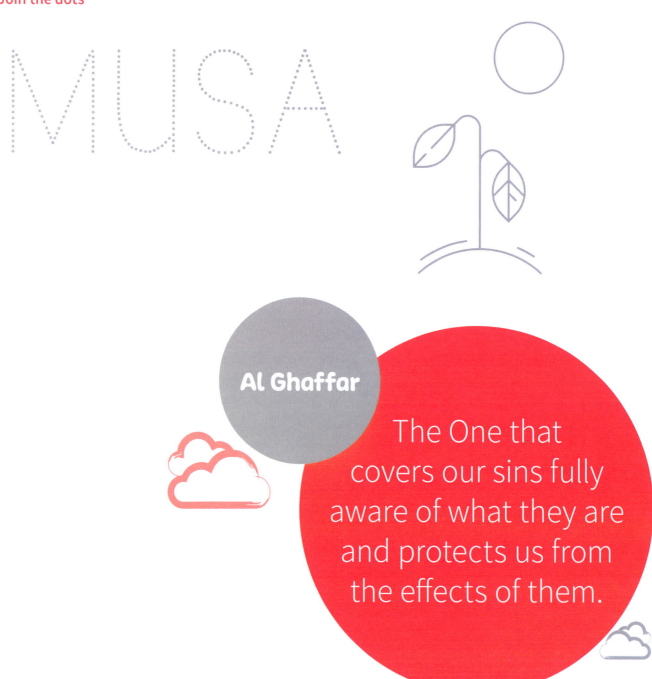

Al Ghaffar

The One that covers our sins fully aware of what they are and protects us from the effects of them.

EPISODE 12

Wordsearch

Tick off the words as you find them

- ◯ MUSA
- ◯ ADAM
- ◯ AL GHAFFAR
- ◯ JANNAH
- ◯ SHAYTAN
- ◯ FORGIVE

M	I	A	J	M	U	S	A	F
U	U	N	E	Z	B	L	O	O
S	R	G	A	L	L	A	S	F
R	L	E	E	J	A	P	H	O
A	L	G	H	A	F	F	A	R
P	D	S	Z	N	Y	U	Y	G
N	R	A	N	N	M	L	T	I
S	A	A	M	A	E	A	A	V
B	N	S	Y	H	L	L	N	E

Al Qahhar

الْقَهَّار

1. What does Al Qahhar mean?

Circle the correct answer

The Most Powerful

The Most Patient

The Most Merciful

2. Which Prophet was sent to Firawn?

Colour in

MUSA

3. How many Eids are there?

Tick the correct answer

○ 1
○ 3
○ 2

EPISODE 13

4. How can we thank Allah?

Colour in

By saying Alhamdulilah

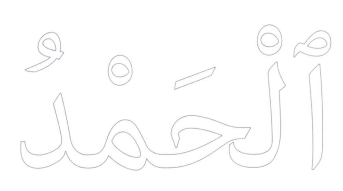

5. Al Wahhab is the one who gifts?

Colour in the correct answer

TRUE

FALSE

6. What were the names of Prophet Ibrahim's sons?

_____

_____

Don't forget to colour in your badge on completion of this worksheet

7. What was the name of the water that sprung up in the story?
Join the dots

ZAMZAM

Al Qahhar

He has power and control over all things and nothing occurs except what He allows.

EPISODE 13

Wordsearch

Tick off the words as you find them

- ○ ZAMZAM
- ○ HAJAR
- ○ ISMAIL
- ○ IBRAHIM
- ○ ISHAQ
- ○ EID

Z	H	Z	H	N	L	P	H	Z
A	A	R	A	K	P	T	A	J
M	L	M	J	M	A	W	I	R
N	U	R	A	P	Z	I	L	Z
N	A	Y	R	T	R	I	E	A
A	R	I	B	R	A	H	I	M
H	E	S	B	M	I	A	T	Z
H	A	I	S	H	A	Q	A	A
B	A	I	D	H	A	L	I	M

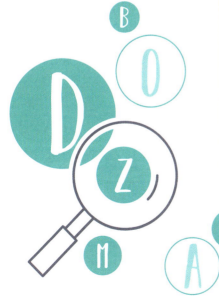

Ar Razzaq

1. What does Ar Razzaq mean?

Circle the correct answer

The One who Creates

The One who Provides Everything

The One who Protects

2. Who ran up and down Mount Safa & Marwa?
Colour in

HAJAR

3. Who put Prophet Yusuf in the well?
Write the answer and colour in

_____

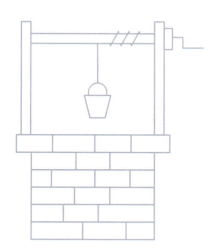

EPISODE 14

4. Write two things you make dua for.

_____

_____

_____

5. Draw a picture to show what charity is.

6. When you give in charity, Allah will give you more in return?

Colour in the correct answer

TRUE

FALSE

7. When you do one good thing, how many rewards do you get minimum?

Tick the correct answer

- ○ 1
- ○ 5
- ○ 10

Ar Razzaq

Allah gives all of His creatures what they can benefit from and what they need to survive.

Wordsearch

Tick off the words as you find them

- ○ CHARITY
- ○ YUSUF
- ○ AR RAZZAQ
- ○ HAJAR
- ○ DUA
- ○ ALLAH

C	I	C	J	M	U	A	D	F
H	U	N	H	Z	B	L	O	A
S	R	G	A	A	L	A	S	L
H	L	D	E	J	R	P	H	L
H	L	G	U	A	F	I	A	A
A	D	S	Z	A	Y	U	T	H
J	R	A	N	N	M	L	T	Y
A	R	R	A	Z	Z	A	Q	V
R	N	S	Y	U	S	U	F	E

Al Fattah

1. Al Fattah means Allah will make things easy for us?

Colour in the correct answer

TRUE

FALSE

2. The name of Prophet Eesa's mother is?

Join the dots

MARIAM

3. Mariam's Uncle was called?

_____
_____

4. Should we ever stop making dua even if we don't get what we want?

Colour in the correct answer

YES | NO

EPISODE 15

5. Which two were the Prophet Muhammad's ﷺ best friends?

Tick the correct answer

- ◯ Umar
- ◯ Ali
- ◯ Uthman
- ◯ Talha
- ◯ Julaybib
- ◯ Abu Bakr

6. The first thing Allah will ask us about is?

Circle the correct answer

Our prayer

Our charity

Our fasting

7. Who writes our book of deeds?

Write the answer and colour in

_____

Don't forget to colour in your badge on completion of this worksheet

8. Which hand do we want to receive our book in?

Write the answer and colour in

_____

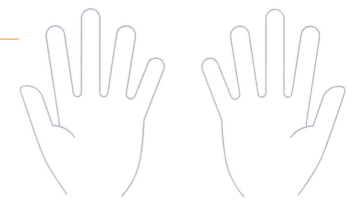

Al Fattah

Allah can open a way for us to get what will benefit us. He can open a way even when it seems impossible!

EPISODE 15

Wordsearch

Tick off the words as you find them

- ⭘ MARIAM
- ⭘ EESA
- ⭘ ZAKARIYAH
- ⭘ UMAR
- ⭘ ABU BAKR
- ⭘ AL FATTAH

A	A	L	F	A	T	T	A	H
B	A	R	U	K	P	T	A	J
U	L	M	J	M	A	Y	I	R
B	U	R	U	P	I	I	L	O
N	A	M	A	R	I	A	M	M
A	R	I	A	A	A	H	I	U
H	E	K	K	R	I	A	T	M
H	A	B	U	B	A	K	R	A
Z	Z	E	E	S	A	L	I	M

Al Aleem

1. What does Al Aleem mean?

Circle the correct answer

Allah is all Forgiving

Allah is all Seeing

Allah is all Knowing

2. Does Allah know what we think about?

Colour in the correct answer

YES | NO

3. Write a dua that you learnt from this episode.

_____
_____
_____

4. How many times do we pray a day?

Tick the correct answer

○ 5
○ 10
○ 3

EPISODE 16

5. What is the reward for saying the dua after wudu?

_____

_____

6. Al Hafeez means Allah does not forget?

Colour in the correct answer

7. Which Prophet hid in a cave from the Quraysh ?

Colour in

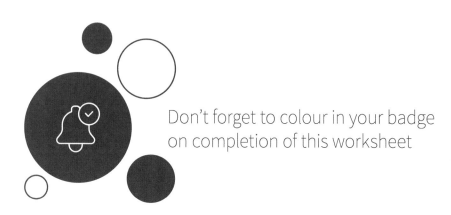

Don't forget to colour in your badge on completion of this worksheet

8. What should we recite after we finish praying?
Join the dots

AYATUL KURSI

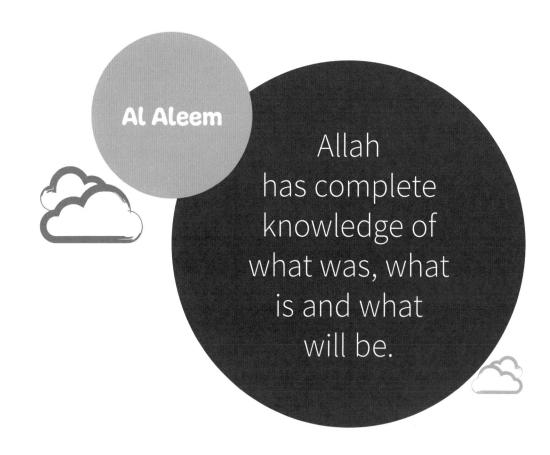

Al Aleem

Allah has complete knowledge of what was, what is and what will be.

EPISODE 16

Wordsearch

Tick off the words as you find them

- ◯ WUDU
- ◯ JANNAH
- ◯ AL ALEEM
- ◯ AL HAFEEZ
- ◯ PROPHET
- ◯ DUA

C	A	C	J	M	U	W	D	F
H	U	L	H	D	B	L	O	E
S	R	G	H	U	L	L	A	H
H	L	D	U	A	R	P	H	L
H	U	D	E	L	F	I	A	P
A	U	A	L	A	L	E	E	M
W	R	A	N	N	M	L	E	Y
A	J	A	N	N	A	H	Q	Z
P	R	O	P	H	E	T	F	E

At Tawaab

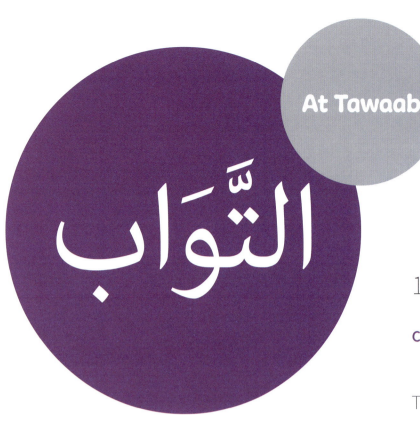

التَّوَّاب

1. At Tawaab refers to...

Circle the correct answer

The One that Forgives

The One that Protects

The One that Creates

2. How can we ask Allah for forgiveness?

_____
_____
_____

3. Which Prophet ate from a tree by mistake?

Write the answer and colour in

_____

4. Which day of the week did this happen on?

Tick the correct answer

◯ Monday
◯ Thursday
◯ Friday

EPISODE 17

5. In the story of the man that killed 100 people where did he end up?

Colour in the correct answer

6. Why was he saved?

_____

_____

_____

_____

Don't forget to colour in your badge on completion of this worksheet

8. Why did the last person to enter Jannah get removed from Jahanum?

Write the answer and colour in

_____

At Tawaab — Allah protects His slaves from things that could hurt them. He protects all creatures by giving them everything they need.

EPISODE 17

Wordsearch

Tick off the words as you find them

- ( ) AT TAWAAB
- ( ) FRIDAY
- ( ) JANNAH
- ( ) DUA
- ( ) JAHANUM
- ( ) FORGIVE

J	A	H	A	N	U	M	F	F
F	A	T	U	K	P	T	R	O
U	L	M	T	J	A	Y	I	R
B	U	R	U	A	I	I	D	G
F	O	F	J	N	W	A	A	I
A	R	R	A	N	A	A	Y	V
H	O	K	K	A	I	A	A	E
F	O	O	U	H	A	K	R	B
F	Z	D	S	S	A	L	I	M

The Azharis | Names of Allah 73

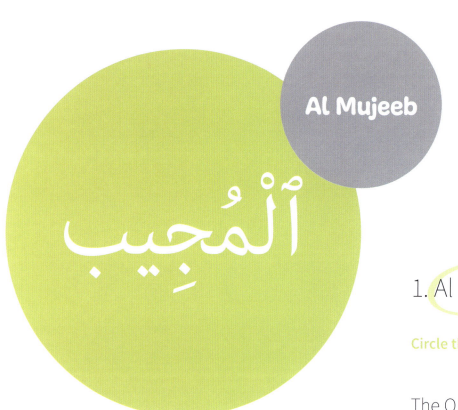

Al Mujeeb

اَلْمُجِيبِ

1. Al Mujeeb refers to...
Circle the correct answer

The One that Answers our duas

The One that Hears our duas

The One that Sees our duas

2. What animal did Prophet Salih's people want?
Write the answer and colour in

_____

3. What did they do to it?

_____
_____
_____

EPISODE 18

4. Is it good to make fun of people?

Colour in the correct answer

5. What was the punishment that happened to them?

_____
_____
_____
_____

6. Is Allah able to answer anyones duas?

Join the dots

Don't forget to colour in your badge on completion of this worksheet

7. What times are best to make dua?

_____
_____
_____
_____

Al Mujeeb

Allah loves to be asked. He is the only One who can give anything you ask for.

EPISODE 18

Wordsearch

Tick off the words as you find them

- ○ SALIH
- ○ AL MUJEEB
- ○ CAMEL
- ○ DUA
- ○ PROPHET
- ○ QURAN

C	P	R	J	M	S	W	Q	F
P	U	Q	U	R	A	N	O	E
S	R	G	H	P	L	L	A	H
H	L	O	S	A	I	P	H	L
H	U	D	P	L	H	I	A	D
A	U	A	E	H	L	P	E	U
A	L	M	U	J	E	E	B	A
A	A	A	N	N	A	T	Q	Z
C	R	A	E	H	E	T	F	E

Al Kareem

الْكَرِيمِ

2. Draw a picture and give us an example of how you can be kind.

1. What does Al Kareem mean?

Circle the correct answer

The Most Merciful

The Most Forgiving

The Most Kind

3. How many good deeds minimum is there for praying 5 times a day?

Tick the correct answer

◯ 10
◯ 30
◯ 100
◯ 50

4. If you do a bad thing how many bad deeds do you get?

Tick the correct answer

○ 3
○ 1
○ 10
○ 2

5. Who used to win the competition Abu Bakr or Umar?

Colour in the correct answer

6. Angels came to the house of which Prophet?

Join the dots and colour in

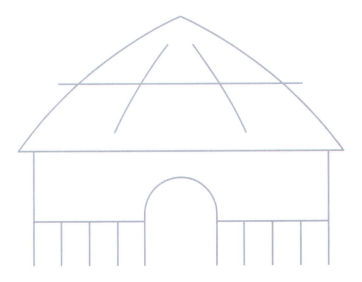

Don't forget to colour in your badge on completion of this worksheet

7. Is it good to share?

Colour in the correct answer

YES | NO

Al Kareem

Allah gives blessings to His creation, even if they do not worship him. His generosity and greatness are limitless.

Wordsearch

Tick off the words as you find them

- ○ AL KAREEM
- ○ IBRAHIM
- ○ KIND
- ○ ABU BAKR
- ○ UMAR
- ○ SALAH

I	L	K	I	N	U	R	S	I
B	A	T	U	K	K	T	R	B
U	L	M	S	A	L	A	H	R
B	U	R	B	A	I	I	P	A
F	O	U	J	E	W	A	A	H
A	B	R	A	N	A	A	Y	I
A	L	K	A	R	E	E	M	M
F	O	O	U	H	A	K	R	M
F	Z	D	U	M	A	R	I	M

Ar Rub

الرَّبّ

1. What does Ar Rub mean?

Circle the correct answer

The One that Looks After

The One that Forgives

The One that is Generous

2. Write a dua you know starting with Rab.

_____
_____
_____
_____
_____
_____
_____

3. What was the first surah to be revealed?

Join the dots

IQRA

EPISODE 20

4. What was the name of Prophet Musa's brother?

Colour in

5. Draw and write a good deed you can do as a family?

6. What caught Prophet Adam when he was running away?

Write the answer and colour in

Don't forget to colour in your badge on completion of this worksheet

Remember to download your certificate of completion for 20 worksheets from theazharis.com

4. What was the name of Prophet Adam's wife?

Colour in

HAWAA

Ar Rub

Allah is Ar Rub. This means He is the only One that creates, nurtures and takes care of His creation.

Wordsearch

Tick off the words as you find them

- ○ ADAM
- ○ HAWAA
- ○ HARUN
- ○ IQRA
- ○ AR RUB
- ○ QURAN

C	H	R	J	A	H	W	A	H
P	A	Q	Q	R	A	N	D	E
Q	R	G	H	P	W	L	A	H
H	U	O	A	A	I	P	H	L
H	U	R	W	L	H	I	A	I
A	U	A	A	D	A	M	E	Q
A	R	M	A	N	E	E	B	R
A	A	R	R	U	B	T	Q	A
C	R	A	E	H	A	R	U	N

EPISODE 20

Al Lateef

اللَّطِيفُ

1. What does Al Lateef mean?

Circle the correct answer

The Most Forgiving

The Most Kind

The Most Gentle

2. Which Prophet was thrown into a well?

Write the answer and colour in

_____

3. Which Prophet did Firawn want to kill?

Join the dots

MUSA

EPISODE 21

4. How did Allah tell Musa to speak to Firawn?

_____
_____
_____

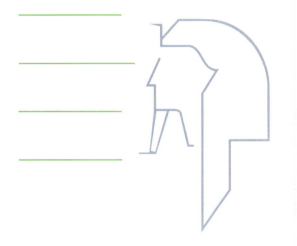

5. Is it good to shout?

Colour in the correct answer

6. Pleasing Allah is by pleasing other people, draw a picture and let us know who you can please.

Don't forget to colour in your badge on completion of this worksheet

7. What happened when Prophet Muhammad ﷺ went to the mountain?

_____
_____
_____
_____

Al Lateef

Allah is knowledgeable of the smallest of matters. Nothing can be hidden from Him, He is aware of all thoughts, hopes and secrets.

EPISODE 21

Wordsearch

Tick off the words as you find them

- ○ YUSUF
- ○ AL LATEEF
- ○ SOFT
- ○ ALLAH
- ○ PARENTS
- ○ WELL

W	Y	Y	I	N	U	W	S	I
B	U	U	U	S	O	F	T	F
U	L	S	S	A	L	A	E	R
B	U	U	B	A	I	E	P	A
W	O	F	J	E	T	A	A	H
A	B	R	A	A	L	L	A	H
A	L	K	L	R	E	E	M	E
F	O	L	U	H	W	E	L	L
P	A	R	E	N	T	S	I	M

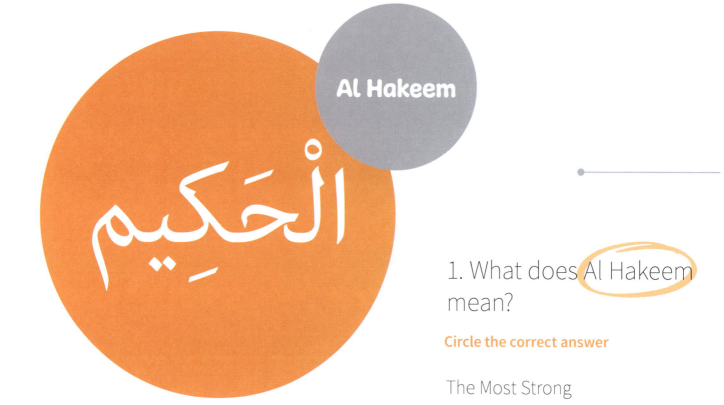

Al Hakeem

1. What does Al Hakeem mean?

Circle the correct answer

The Most Strong

The Most Kind

The Most Wise

2. Which month was the Quran revealed in?

Colour in

3. Draw a picture and let us know what you would like to eat in Jannah?

EPISODE 22

4. About how many good deeds are there in reciting Ayatul Kursi?

Tick the correct answer

◯ 100
◯ 2200
◯ 1900

5. What is the smallest animal you can think of?

_____

_____

_____

_____

6. How can we protect ourselves from Shaytan at night?

Write the asnwer and colour in

_____

_____

_____

Don't forget to colour in your badge on completion of this worksheet

7. Can Allah forgive us no matter how many mistakes we make?
Colour in the correct answer

YES | NO

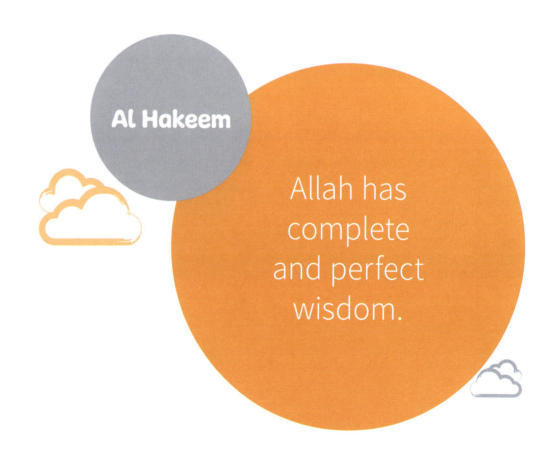

Al Hakeem

Allah has complete and perfect wisdom.

EPISODE 22

Wordsearch

Tick off the words as you find them

- ○ AL HAKEEM
- ○ RAMADAN
- ○ SHAYTAN
- ○ JANNAH
- ○ ALLAH
- ○ IMAM

C	S	R	S	A	J	W	A	H
P	H	Q	A	L	I	N	D	E
R	A	G	L	L	W	M	N	H
H	Y	O	S	A	I	A	A	L
H	T	A	W	H	D	I	A	M
A	A	L	H	A	K	E	E	M
A	N	M	M	N	E	E	B	I
A	A	A	R	U	B	T	Q	A
C	R	A	J	A	N	N	A	H

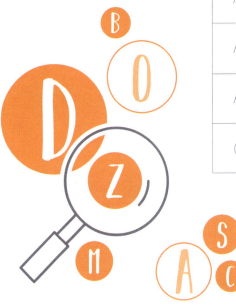

The Azharis | Names of Allah 93

As Samee

السَّمِيع

1. What does As Samee mean?

Circle the correct answer

The All Seeing

The All Knowing

The All Hearing

2. What is more important, listening or speaking?

_____

3. Let us know what you have made dua for?

_____
_____
_____
_____
_____

EPISODE 23

4. If your dua is not answered straight away, do you stop making dua?

Colour in the correct answer

 |

5. Where is the Kabah?

_____

_____

7. How can we thank Allah?

_____

_____

_____

6. Which Prophet built the Kabah with his son?

Join the dots

Don't forget to colour in your badge on completion of this worksheet

8. The more you thank Allah the more he will give you?

Colour in the correct answer

TRUE

FALSE

As Samee

Allah hears every word and every sound. He hears anything that can be heard. He hears even the quietest whisper.

EPISODE 23

Wordsearch

Tick off the words as you find them

- ○ AS SAMEE
- ○ KABAH
- ○ MECCA
- ○ IBRAHIM
- ○ SHUKR
- ○ DUA

A	S	K	I	D	I	M	S	I
S	U	A	M	S	H	F	T	M
I	I	B	R	A	H	I	M	E
S	U	U	B	A	I	E	E	A
H	M	F	J	K	T	M	A	H
U	E	R	A	A	A	L	A	H
K	C	K	L	S	E	B	M	E
R	C	L	S	H	D	U	A	L
P	A	A	E	N	T	S	I	H

Al Haleem

الْحَلِيم

1. What does Al Haleem mean?

Circle the correct answer

The Most Kind

The Most Gentle

The Most Patient

2. Does Allah punish us straight away if we do something bad?

Colour in the correct answer

3. Write an example of being generous to someone.

_____
_____
_____
_____

EPISODE 24

4. What does being merciful mean?

Join the dots

5. What was the name of the angel that came to the Prophet Muhammad ﷺ in the cave?

Tick the correct answer

- ○ Jibril
- ○ Israfil
- ○ Mikail

6. Who did the Prophet Muhammad ﷺ go to?

Colour in

KHADIJAH

Don't forget to colour in your badge on completion of this worksheet

7. Write the story of Taif.

_____

_____

_____

_____

_____

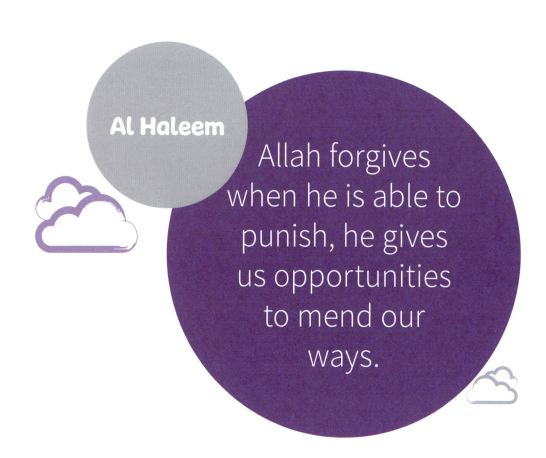

Al Haleem

Allah forgives when he is able to punish, he gives us opportunities to mend our ways.

EPISODE 24

Wordsearch

Tick off the words as you find them

- ○ AL HALEEM
- ○ SABR
- ○ GENEROUS
- ○ JIBRIL
- ○ TAIF
- ○ CAVE

J	G	R	S	S	J	G	A	C
P	H	Q	F	L	S	N	D	E
C	E	I	L	C	A	V	E	V
H	A	O	S	A	B	A	A	L
T	G	E	N	E	R	O	U	S
T	A	L	P	A	K	T	E	A
A	L	H	A	L	E	E	M	B
A	A	A	R	U	B	T	Q	R
C	R	A	J	I	B	R	I	L

The Azharis | Names of Allah 101

Ar Raqeeb

الرَّقِيب

1. What does Ar Raqeeb mean?

Circle the correct answer

The All Hearing

The All Knowing

The All Observing

2. If you hide can Allah still see you?

Colour in the correct answer

YES | NO

3. Which companion was mentioned in story time today?

Colour in

UMAR

EPISODE 25

4. What happened when Umar asked for a sheep?

_____
_____
_____

5. What do you say when you meet someone?

Colour in

اَلسَّلَامُ عَلَيْكُم

6. What happens when you shake hands?

Write the answer and colour in

_____
_____
_____

Don't forget to colour in your badge on completion of this worksheet

7. Why did the last man in the story keep his sheep?
Write the answer and colour in

_____

_____

_____

Ar Raqeeb

Allah closely watches over his creation. He hears, sees and knows everything and nothing can escape him.

EPISODE 25

Wordsearch

Tick off the words as you find them

- ⃝ TRUTH
- ⃝ AR RAQEEB
- ⃝ UMAR
- ⃝ SHEEP
- ⃝ ALLAH
- ⃝ MUSLIM

A	R	K	I	T	I	M	S	I
S	T	A	L	S	H	F	R	S
A	R	R	A	Q	E	E	B	E
S	U	U	B	A	I	E	E	A
H	T	F	M	K	T	M	A	P
M	H	R	A	A	A	L	E	H
U	E	K	L	O	R	E	M	E
A	L	L	A	H	H	P	A	L
P	S	M	U	S	L	I	M	H

Al Wadud

الْوَدُودُ

1. Al Wadud refers to?

Circle the correct answer

The One that Hates

The One that Loves

The One that Likes

2. Write down one thing that Allah loves?

_____

3. What is Ihsan?

_____
_____
_____
_____

4. Can you give an example of being patient?

EPISODE 26

5. What is the name of Prophet Yusuf's dad?

Colour in

6. Which Prophet did Allah tell to leave his wife and son in the desert?

Join the dots

7. What did this Prophet say when he was thrown into a fire and Jibril came?

_____

_____

_____

_____

Don't forget to colour in your badge on completion of this worksheet

8. How many rakat is Maghrib?

Tick the correct answer

- ◯ 3
- ◯ 4
- ◯ 2
- ◯ 1

Al Wadud

His love to His slaves includes being merciful to them and accepting their deeds.

EPISODE 26

Wordsearch

Tick off the words as you find them

- ○ AL WADUD
- ○ MAGHRIB
- ○ YAQUB
- ○ IBRAHIM
- ○ IHSAN
- ○ JIBRIL

M	Y	A	I	S	J	G	A	I
P	I	B	R	A	H	I	M	E
A	L	W	A	D	U	D	E	V
J	A	J	S	A	B	A	Y	N
I	G	I	N	E	R	O	A	S
B	A	B	P	A	K	S	Q	A
R	L	R	A	L	H	E	U	B
I	A	I	R	I	B	T	B	R
L	M	A	G	H	R	I	B	L

Al Waasi

الْوَاسِعِ

1. Al Waasi refers to?

Circle the correct answer

The One without any difuculty

The One overlooking

The One in charge

2. Give an example of how Allah is merciful to us?

_____

_____

3. Which Prophet was sent to the Bani Israel?
Colour in

EPISODE 27

4. Who had the sling shot?

Join the dots

DAWUD

5. What happened?

_____
_____
_____
_____

6. Is giving in charity good?

Write the answer and colour in

_____
_____
_____

7. Will we be poor if we give in charity?

Colour in the correct answer

YES

NO

8. Why did Shaytan not like Prophet Adam?

_____

_____

_____

Al Waasi

Allah accomodates the prayers of His creation and does not hold them responsible for what is beyond their capabilities.

EPISODE 27

Wordsearch

Tick off the words as you find them

- ○ AL WAASI
- ○ RAHMA
- ○ MUSA
- ○ DAWUD
- ○ CHARITY
- ○ SHAYTAN

A	S	C	R	T	I	M	S	I
S	H	A	Y	T	A	N	R	S
A	R	R	A	Q	L	E	B	C
S	K	U	B	A	W	E	D	H
H	T	F	M	K	A	M	A	A
M	H	H	A	R	A	A	W	R
U	A	K	L	O	S	P	U	I
R	L	L	A	U	I	P	D	T
P	S	L	M	S	L	I	M	Y

Ar Rauf Al Jami

الرَّؤُوف الْجَامِع

1. Ar Rauf refers to The One who is Most Merciful and Kind?

Colour in the correct answer

TRUE

FALSE

2. Give an example of something we can copy from the Prophet ﷺ?
_____
_____

3. If someone treats us badly, should we treat them badly?

Colour in the correct answer

EPISODE 28

4. Al Jami means?

Circle the correct answer

The One that Gathers

The One Forgives

The One that Loves

5. What is Friday in Arabic?

Join the dots

JUMMAH

6. Will it be hot or cold on the day of judgement?

_____

_____

Don't forget to colour in your badge on completion of this worksheet

7. Name one group who will be shaded on that day?
Write the answer and colour in

_____

_____

_____

Ar Rauf Al Jami

Allah cares about everything and gives mercy to everything and everyone he chooses.

EPISODE 28

Wordsearch

Tick off the words as you find them

- ○ AR RAUF
- ○ AL JAMI
- ○ JUMMAH
- ○ PROPHET
- ○ SHADE
- ○ HADITH

S	J	A	I	P	J	J	A	I
A	J	S	H	A	H	I	P	E
L	L	U	A	D	U	D	R	S
J	A	J	M	A	B	A	O	H
A	G	I	N	M	R	O	P	A
M	A	B	P	A	A	S	H	D
I	L	R	A	L	H	H	E	E
I	A	R	R	A	U	F	T	R
L	M	A	H	A	D	I	T	H

Al Haq

الْحَقُ

1. Al Haq refers to?

Circle the correct answer

The All Seeing

The Absolute Truth

The All Hearing

2. What is the opposite of a lie?

_____

_____

3. What month do we fast in?

Colour in

RAMADAN

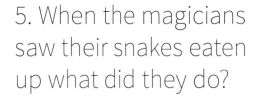

EPISODE 29

4. What happened when Musa threw down his staff?

_____

_____

_____

5. When the magicians saw their snakes eaten up what did they do?

_____

_____

_____

6. What do we recite before going to bed?

Join the dots

Don't forget to colour in your badge on completion of this worksheet

7. Draw a picture and let us know what you would like in Jannah.

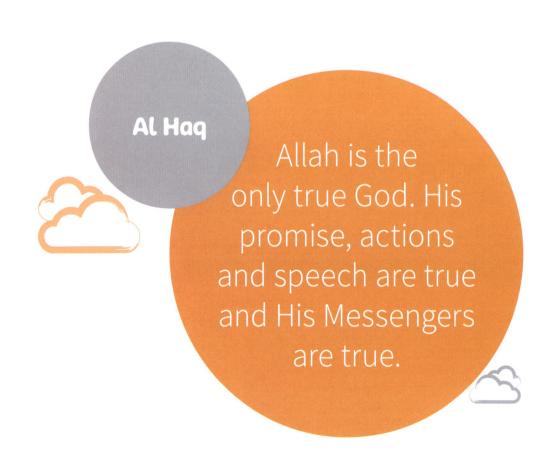

EPISODE 29

Wordsearch

Tick off the words as you find them

- ○ AL HAQ
- ○ RAMADAN
- ○ TRUTH
- ○ MAGICIAN
- ○ STAFF
- ○ SNAKE

A	S	C	T	A	L	M	S	R
S	M	A	G	I	C	I	A	N
R	R	R	A	Q	F	E	B	A
S	K	U	B	F	W	E	D	L
R	A	M	A	D	A	N	A	H
M	H	T	A	R	A	A	T	A
U	S	N	A	K	E	U	U	Q
R	L	L	A	U	R	P	D	T
P	T	L	M	T	L	I	M	Y

The Azharis | Names of Allah 121

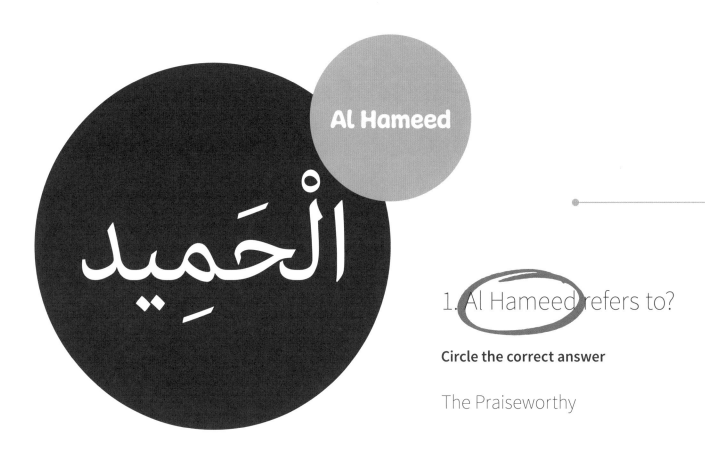

Al Hameed

1. Al Hameed refers to?

Circle the correct answer

The Praiseworthy

The Absolute Truth

The All Knowing

2. What do you say when you praise someone?

Join the dots

MASHAALLAH

3. Everything good comes from?

Colour in

EPISODE 30

4. What does Allahu Akbar mean?

_____

_____

5. Who was Qarun to Musa?

_____

_____

6. Was Qarun good or bad?

Colour in the correct answer

GOOD | BAD

7. What happened to all his treasure?

Write the asnwer and colour in

_____

_____

Don't forget to colour in your badge on completion of this worksheet

Remember to download your certificate of completion for 30 worksheets from theazharis.com

8. Who was Prophet Muhammad's ﷺ best friend?

Colour in

ABU BAKR

Al Hameed

The One that deserves to be praised.

EPISODE 30

Wordsearch

Tick off the words as you find them

- ☐ ALLAH
- ☐ AL HAMEED
- ☐ QARUN
- ☐ MUSA
- ☐ ABU BAKR
- ☐ QURAN

S	A	A	I	P	J	J	A	I
A	A	B	U	B	A	K	R	E
A	L	U	A	Q	U	D	R	Q
L	A	J	M	A	A	A	O	H
L	G	I	Q	M	R	R	P	A
A	A	B	U	A	A	S	U	D
H	L	R	R	L	H	H	E	N
A	L	H	A	M	E	E	D	R
L	M	A	N	A	M	U	S	A

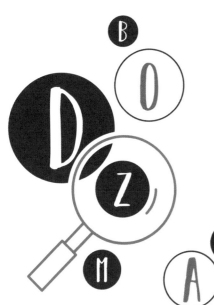

THE AZHARIS

ALSO IN THE SERIES:

Juz by Juz Stories

Who is Allah

Tafsir Surah Al Kahf

Who is Muhammad

www.theazharis.com

Don't forget your
AZHARI DINOSAURS

AZHARI RAPTOR

AZHARIDACTYL

AZHARISAURUS

AZHARI REX

www.theazharis.com

ANSWERS

Episode 01
1. Jannah
2. No
3. Abdullah and Abdul Rahman
4. Fatiha
5. Over 2,000
6. Bismillah

Episode 02
1. Ar Rahman
2. Ar Raheem
3. Being kind
4. -
5. Mercy
6. Being kind
7. Yes
8. Yes
9. Being kind to animals

Episode 03
1. Owner/King
2. Firawn
3. Make dua for you
4. True
5. 33
6. Surah Al Kahf
7. He did not thank Allah
8. Allah

Episode 04
1. The One that Purifies
2. Black
3. No
4. Front
5. No
6. Well/good
7. Musa
8. Your people won't be able to pray that much
9. The One that puts Barakah in things
10. -

Episode 05
1. The Protector
2. Assalamualaykum
3. The one who starts
4. 8
5. -
6. -
7. Friday

Episode 06
1. The One who give Eeman
2. Allah knows everything before it happens
3. -
4. Firawn
5. Asiyah
6. Surah Al Kahf
7. Harun
8. Abu Bakr

Episode 07
1. The One that Protects us
2. Yunus
3. Ibrahim
4. Musa
5. Egypt
6. 5
7. It was too heavy and he had to jump
8. Angels

Episode 08
1. The Most Powerful
2. No
3. Ibrahim
4. Nile
5. Egypt
6. Firawn
7. True
8. Surah Mulk

Episode 09
1. The One that Fixes
2. One
3. No
4. 40 Years
5. Yusha
6. The sun to stop
7. His hand got stuck in Prophet Yusha's

Episode 10
1. The One who is the Greatest
2. Allahuakbar
3. Allah is greater than anything
4. Adam
5. Shaytan
6. Right
7. Yes
8. Soil/Clay

Episode 11
1. The Creator
2. Allah
3. Hearts
4. True
5. Yes
6. True
7. Summer

Episode 12
1. The One who Forgives
2. Ask Allah for forgiveness
3. No
4. Shaytan
5. Adam
6. -
7. Musa

Episode 13
1. The Most Powerful
2. Musa
3. 2
4. Alhamdulilah
5. True
6. Ismail & Ishaq
7. Zamzam

Episode 14
1. The One who Provides Everything
2. Hajar
3. His Brothers
4. -
5. -
6. True
7. 10

Episode 15
1. True
2. Mariam
3. Zakariyah
4. No
5. Abu Bakr & Umar
6. Our prayer
7. Angels
8. Right